The Little Things

Danielle Kogan

BookLeaf
Publishing

India | USA | UK

Presentation by *BookLeaf Publishing*

Web: www.bookleafpub.com

E-mail: info@bookleafpub.com

ISBN: 9789357443913

First edition 2022

DEDICATION

To Juffyn and Pulya, who were both natural masters and teachers of living only in the present.

ACKNOWLEDGEMENT

In what I hope to make a short reel of a compendium of thanks I owe, I'd like to acknowledge the following individuals:

My deepest and most heartfelt thanks go out to Dina and Igor Kogan, who did not let the pressure of being a first-generation American push me into a 'more legitimate' career. Beyond that, I'd like to thank:

Ms. Sandy Faison, Mr. Jonathan Davidson, Mr. Robert Krausz, Mr. Lee Lobehofer, Ms. Stacy Cervellino, Mr. Harry Shifman, Mr. John Lewis, Ms. Elizabeth Healy, Ms. Michelle Kingham Cronin, Dr. Barbara Rowes, and Ms. Lourdes DeLaCruz of the faculty at LaGuardia High School for Music and Art and the Performing Arts;

It was these teachers that showed me art could be something I thread into my life in any capacity if I just allowed myself to lean into it.

Ms. Laura Tesman, Ms. Jolie Tong, Mr. Manuel Simons, Ms. Cristina Duarte, Mr. Jeff Stiefel,

Mr. Michael Hairston, and Ms. Niluka Hotaling
of the Drama Department; and Mr. Don Hecker
& Mr. Anthony Mancini of the Journalism
Department at CUNY-Brooklyn College.

*It was these teachers who demonstrated endless
patience and respect for my work, and allowed
me to grow in kind and safe spaces.*

My beloved thanks also go out to Nadya
Drukker, Rozet Mavashev, and Yelena Azriyel
of the Tanger Hillel and my business partners
Jim Walsh and Samantha Castro, all of whom do
not let work ever get in the way of work that
matters.

PREFACE

Thank you for taking a big chance on this
very-big-deal of a little book!

This Heartbeat

This is not a small and singular heartbeat.

This heartbeat is
The one beating with the fire of 15.2 million
stars, fuelled by every star born prior to those.
The one of
Hannah, Anne, Hedy,
Franceska, and Marianne.
The one of
Esther, Michal, Miriam,
Yocheved, and Zipporah.

This heartbeat is not
One you can quiet for your comfort
One you can force into a different rhythm
One you can ignore in a soundscape

This heartbeat is
Particularly strong when it resists 'fitting in.'
Particularly loud when it is forced into silence.
Particularly steady when it is comforting those
who forgot to hear it.

This heartbeat is not
Something you can contain in your space,

Something you can avoid sensing in your spirit,
Something you can forget knowing in your
mind.

This heartbeat is
Initialed by twenty-two constant letters that do
not change, yet stay open to change.
Drumming too intensely onwards regardless of
whether you believe it should exist.
Unique to the 15.2 million (and counting) that
beat in harmony with it

This is not a small and singular heartbeat.

26 Letters

A million combinations of 26 letters decide
How successfully one will survive
How many people over these graphemes died?

Wiser people than I have sat around and cried
Cultures buried in letters they could not revive,
A million combinations of 26 letters decide

I translated the news for my parents, I tried
Human minds forced into mental overdrive
How many people over these graphemes died?

Whether new doors will open wide.
The difference between living or staying alive
A million combinations of 26 letters decide

Still translating, and lost, and bleary-eyed
So many canceled, forgotten, lost in an archive
How many people over these graphemes died?

These symbols- relentless, Jekyll & Hyde
I wonder what I'll do with them past ninety-five

A million combinations of 26 letters decide
How many people over these graphemes died?

Rain in Los Angeles

There's nothing like a thunderstorm with
lightning and rain
It's a natural and rare sound that quiets my brain
Itching to feel those thunderous vibrations roll
through me
Sploosh around in the weather that people find
gloomy.

So when I wake to the wet, wild symphony of
sound
And I splash my way to breakfast because I
don't run around
I'm reminded I'm alive and my hair is drenched
and dripping
Two cups of hot tea, and soup, then back in the
room I'm stripping

There's no thunder, and no lightning, everyone
else seems upset
But the rain always reveals what was stained and
unwashed yet,
So I'm standing watching droplets race down
window panes and smiling
The voices in the bigger room I hear are very
busy reconciling

How "it sucks that it is raining," but "it's really
not so bad"
"Did somebody bring a bathing suit? For
what?!" And now they're sad,
How they wish it wasn't raining, how they wish
the sun was out
The majority of dampened faces stressed into a
pout.

Oh it poured in California, mid-December, I was
there
I was three whole hours younger, I thought it felt
more than fair
I felt lucky to age backward, and to meet beyond
a screen
To see faces in the sunlight that in theory shared
a dream

It would have all been a dream! I am sure! I am
convinced,
If the whole of California that day didn't get a
rinse-
Then I would have woken up and thought that
none of it was real
And I wouldn't have remembered just how good
'alive' could feel.

Coffee

The world pities busy monsters that have a
million names,
Until they sip from a boiling black bean juice,
and get preoccupied with their

Making and doing and **big-ifying** of their
littleized specialties
Things that **need to happen!!!**
Now-today-by-the-end-of-the-day
-this-afternoon-immediately!
Initially because their **big-ification**
could be <u>very important</u>,
Especially for the future of things that
need to happen!!!

And then when the busy monsters are too
preoccupied with the world they are making,
Not the world they are living in,
With the things they are doing,
Not the way they are doing them,

They flitter about to find
What remains of greenery,
Procure their boiling black bean juice,
Thank what remains of the lucky stars,

The ones they can still see between the steam
from the bean juice and the **big-ifying**

And get back to the
Things that **need to happen!!!**
Now-today-by-the-end-of-the-day
-this-afternoon-immediately!!!

And then, most interestingly:

Those who did not make things that need to
happen (happen) blame the bean water
The having it, or the non-having of it, or the
enough-ness in having it and
Somehow it's all the fault of the bean water

Which if anything has only ever held one name,
Small-ified itself for a billion busy monsters'
benefit.

Woe is the boiling black bean juice doing its best
and still getting blamed for things it isn't doing.

Cardboard Slabs

I am loud, in person, and in presence.
I am 5'3" and ¾ of an inch last time I check and
I am hard-to-not-see and in color and carbonated
and
I am all these things that few people, and places,
and things have ever been able to prove
otherwise.

I am nothing but a sore throat from being forced
to stay so loud and sustaining being so
hard-to-not-see.

I am carrying my heart-holding half with my
shoelace legs to a magic place.

The be-yourself-and-quiet-and
-not-the-thing-people-notice place.

And my big brain, which has much like
anyone's, full of
Soundproofing between the wrinkles that makes
sure no one else can hear
What we're thinking
Hears a big think!
(and then finally silence when I walk in.)

I am opening a world between
Two slabs of cardboard and then *shwoop*!
I have disappeared into it, and
I am still reading, all 5'3" and ¾ of me
(last I checked)
I am in color and carbonated and running my
Eyes along the blots between
Two slabs of cardboard
When it hits me

I am from the Earth and so is everything that
Built the world between two magical slabs of
cardboard
The one I jumped into where I was only seeing,
And not overseeing (thankfully).

I am in the library,
I am with a new book, and
I love it here.

8 Things I Used to Think

I used to think that
The car had magic powers
Streets moved under it.

I used to think that
If I ate the seeds of fruit
Trees would grow in me.

I used to think that
People on Earth's other side
All walked upside down.

I used to think that
If chocolate made you happy
Tons of it can't hurt

I used to think that
Mean people were born so mean
And grew mean people

          I used to think that
          Bodies only listened and
          Never ever talked back.

I used to think that
Cat food was tastier, cause
My cat ate wildly

          I used to think that
          Growing up was so scary
          Feels good to be wrong.

Kiss Me, Pretty Please

Kindergartener,
  that's what I'm acting like when
I ask you to kiss me
  don't make me ask you,
So innocently, nuzzling into the nape of your
  neck and then
So abrasively, glaring at you and daring you not
  to do it.
Madwoman, that's what I'm
  becoming
Every time there's too long a time without
  seeing you.
Pretty please? You know what it does to me, it
  quiets the
Racket and ridiculousness of the conversations
  going on between my ears
Every second of every day
  otherwise
The audaciousness of
  you...
The way you cup
  my face...
You are strong and gentle and safe and mine.
  (which is hard to believe)

Preposterous, that's what you are- respectfully,
          how dare you?
Letting me go unkissed throughout the day, pfft,
          you are
Egregious as an adult, especially in the moments
          that you are not kissing me.
And I am all set to throw a full-blown tantrum
          about it, but it
Sinks away into the depths of
          my mind
Every time you end up going for it.

My Fibonaccis

Golden

You

Your geometries

I imagine it

Probably as close to God-like

As anything human can ever get and honestly,

Watching this world spin around and about you-
that makes the most sense.

The most beautiful numbers in the world will be
generated with your coming, I can tell already,
there won't be enough.

Time and tools and languages to tell and show
and reassure you that's the case, although I hope
you'll never need that kind of reassurance. I
hope you realize your power slowly and then-

All at once, like falling asleep. The ratio of you
to me comes in perfect timing, and even though
you are not an idea yet, or even a seed of an
idea, I can sense you coming. You all visit my
dreams, I worry signaling your arrival too soon,
but this can be our secret.

In Response To
How I'm Feeling

I wonder if I'll operate permanently in a state of low-grade anxiety. This seems to be the natural state of being for most people between the ages of 18 and 28. And, since January of this year, finding:

Five things to see,
Four things to touch,
Three things to hear,
Two things to smell, and,
One thing to taste;

Becomes useless when I cannot smell anything that isn't overwhelming and even then I can just barely.
Shocks me that New York City is not as overwhelmingly smelly as I thought, it should have helped.
Shocks me that switching the numbers around, tasting an extra snack- it does not help the same way.

In fact, all it does is draw attention to the reality that:

Five things look incredibly
fuzzy without my glasses,
Four things I touch I barely register because I
am cold and often do not feel my toes,
Three things I hear include the music in my
head, which is also distracting
And beyond that all I notice is that I am
probably overeating
As well as
 chronically dehydrated.

I wonder if having lost my sense of smell
translates into having lost my sense of security.
I wonder if both come back at once the way your
soul does when you wake up, and
I wonder if being between the ages of 18 and 28
is mostly made up of wondering about
the little things.

And now, all I have got left is:

Five trillion thoughts in
Four milliseconds in
Three and a half languages all at once with
Two seconds total to choose from and answer
One singular question:

"So, how are you feeling today?"

Favorite Sounds

I love hearing genuine laughter
And I love the silence right after

Like champagne in the ears;
It feels best when with peers;

The hearing of genuine laughter.

I love hearing an audience fall silent
Before crowds of applause get so violent

Thunder almost can't beat
Whoops and stomps for the for the feat;

Post a show where an audience falls silent.

I love hearing rain against our roof
I dance around to its drumbeat, aloof

There's all kinds of rhythm
In life's algorithm

I live to hear rain against our roof

I love to hear wind rustle tree leaves
The tickle of its noisiness against my knees

With a whisper and a breath
Leaves go flying with breadth

With the sound of wind rustling in tree leaves.

The Logic of Little Idioms

Also Known As
**Mostly Logical Poetry for
Mostly Logical People**

If hurt people hurt people,
  then healed people heal people, so:

If you are hanging in there,
  then you must be getting strong!

If it has gotten out of hand,
  then you could hold somebody else's, and

If you happen to miss the boat,
  I'm sure the train will come along.

If you seek a needle in a haystack,
  get to looking when it's light out,

If you have spoken of the devil,
  it makes sense that you feel warm.

If you are sent back the drawing board,
  there must be an idea coming,

If there's an act that got together,
  then actors are in proper form.

If you're pulling someone's leg,
  then be nice- make sure they stretch,

If you're caught under the weather,
  it makes sense that you would kvetch.

If you've pulled yourself together,
  better tie yourself securely,

If easy does it,
  then hard does not, and

If it's so far so good, then
  so good so far it must be, surely.

The Way He Trots

He trotted along, a pink tongue hanging-
With button eyes and a teddy-bear nose.
A non-horse non-bear has my heart clanging!
He trotted along, a pink tongue hanging-
The way his voice had my ears banging.
I'll never forget his fifth position pose.
He trots along, a pink tongue hanging,
With button eyes and a teddy-bear nose.

Her Majesty's Rispetto

I miss your very soft, fluffy, lengthy tail
I miss your knowing look, which levels all men
I miss your purrs and protests, and without fail
I check the spaces you hid now and again
Your memory is much much crueler than you
Doubly that on occasions when I am blue
Nobody misses you, no, not quite like me,
And you were such a big part of our family.

The Word Not

People are no good at saying
what they are
But they are very good at knowing
what they're not.
People are terrible at sensing
when they're right
But if you ask them when they're wrong,
they're flabbergasted on the spot.

People are atrocious at thinking for themselves
And good at not thinking most things through
completely, or at all.
People are horrendous at not saying they don't
know things,
And they're wonderful at asking if you are ok
when you bawl.

People are not kind if they are hungry or afraid,
Or anything that bugs them, like being hot, or
cold,
People are not innocent once they have gotten
laid,
Or once they have lived a life and consider
themselves 'old.'

People are not willing, not trying, or not there
People are across the world accusing those who
do not care,
People are forget-me-not-ing and do not sleep a
wink
People swear not-on-my-life, and who are
challenged not to blink,

All these people, all this nonsense
Over negatives and not being,
They are all last, but all not least
In the world of what I'm seeing.

Little Lies

"I've only had a few drinks, and I'm fine."
"I'm only five minutes away!"
"I'm in the most terrible traffic!"
"My phone died! What did you say?"

"Of course I remember you!"
"No, really, the outfit looks great."
"I'm never on social media."
"Holy cow, have you lost weight?"

"I am so sorry to miss it!"
"No, that really is not too much!"
"Oh goodness, what a cute baby!"
"For sure, let's keep in touch."

"My goodness, that tasted delicious."
"I'm on the edge of my seat in suspense."
"Oh no, that doesn't seem suspicious."
"Oh yeah, it makes perfect sense."

My Grandmother's Soup

Strength returns to me
The heat lights my fiery spirit
My spiky throat drenched
In heavy hot broth
I am getting well.

Tongue Twisters and Subsequent Translated Thoughts from a Foriegn Language

I'm learning English and annunciation
Near the poster with the
Picture of a train station.

We're sitting on a carpet learning
Tongue twisters
I'm busy picking at my blisters.

She sees cheese.
And nobody asked her what she did with it,
which is weird.

A happy hippo hopped and hiccupped.
And you wonder if hippos share the same
cultural way of getting rid of their hiccups.

Twelve twins twirled twelve twigs.
And you wonder if the twins are particularly
small and what their mom is like.

I scream, you scream, we all scream for ice cream.
And you wonder if screaming is common in American culture (it is).

Round and round the rugged rocks the ragged rascal ran.
At some point, he probably looked lean, which everybody lately seems concerned about becoming, so good for him.

The thirty-three thieves thought that they thrilled the throne throughout Thursday.
And you think they must have been pardoned if they're entertaining in a throne room.

Six sick hicks nick six slick bricks with picks and sticks.
Don't they have better things to do?

Lucky rabbits like to cause a ruckus.
And here I thought rabbits were ruckus-like in general- what a misconception.

Oy Vey!

Did something break?
Oy Vey!
Did somebody do something dumb?
Oy Vey!
Did somebody die?
Oy Vey!
Did somebody leave the table with crumbs?
Oy Vey!

Did someone annoy you?
Oy Vey!
Did something rip open a shirt?
Oy Vey!
Did you go outside without wet hair?
Oy Vey!
Did you come back covered in dirt?
Oy Vey!

Did you wake your mother in the middle of the
night?
Oy Vey!
Did you tickle your sister and get kicked?
Oy Vey!
Did your aunt caked in makeup kiss your cheek?
Oy Vey!

Did your dog wet your face when he licked?
Oy Vey!

Did you fail a test?
Oy Vey!
Did you cry over a boy?
Oy Vey!
Did you lose the power of speech?
Oy Vey!
Well, when you don't know what to say-

Oy Vey!

Socks

Toasty toes have never been happier,
And their ability to wiggle was never snappier!!
Who doesn't have warm socks has frigid feet.
And won't tap quite as well to a given beat.

Sunlight

So, my favorite way to wake up is
Under the covers sunlight on my face
Never is there a feeling as
Laugh-inducing, and when it happens that way,
Immediately, all I know is I
Giggle and my whole body
Heats up and fuels me to stretch until I am ready
To start the day- this is officially sweet morning.

Hello!

"Hello!"

says the smiling stranger
         who lives in the world's
                   meanest city.

"Hello!"

I say, smiling back.
         It's not all bad,
                   it can be pretty.